TORONTO PUBLIC LIBRARY

WITHDRAWN
FROM NORTH YORK PUBLIC LIBRARY

D1308774

Author:

Ian Graham studied applied physics at the City University, London. He then took a postgraduate degree in journalism, specialising in science and technology. Since becoming a freelance author and journalist, he has written more than one hundred children's non-fiction books.

Artist:

David Antram was born in Brighton, England, in 1958. He studied at Eastbourne College of Art and then worked in advertising for fifteen years before becoming a full-time artist. He has illustrated many children's non-fiction books.

Series creator:
David Salariya

Editor:
Michael Ford

© The Salariya Book Company Ltd MMIV
All rights reserved. No part of this book may be reproduced, stored in a retrieval system or transmitted in any form or by any means, electronic, mechanical, photocopying, recording or otherwise, without the written permission of the copyright owner.

Published in Great Britain in 2004 by
Book House, an imprint of
The Salariya Book Company Ltd
25 Marlborough Place, Brighton BN1 1UB

Please visit the Salariya Book Company at:
www.salariya.com

ISBN 1 904642 54 3

A catalogue record for this book is available from the British Library.
Printed and bound in China.
Printed on paper from sustainable forests.

Visit our website at **www.book-house.co.uk**
for free electronic versions of:
You wouldn't want to be an Egyptian Mummy!
You wouldn't want to be a Roman Gladiator!
Avoid joining Shackleton's Polar Expedition!

Curie

and the science of radioactivity

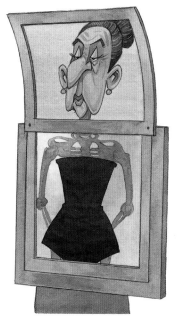

Written by
Ian Graham

Illustrated by
David Antram

The Explosion Zone

BOOK HOUSE

Contents

Introduction 5

A Polish girl 6

Invisible rays 8

A mystery element 10

A witch's brew 12

Getting to know radium 14

The radium craze 16

Blisters and burns 18

Spreading the word 20

Tragedy! 22

The 'Little Curies' 24

Welcome to America 26

The end of the story 28

Glossary 30

Index 32

Introduction

On 7th November, 1867, Marya Sklodovska was born in Warsaw, Poland, which was ruled by Russia at that time. When the Russian authorities banned laboratory studies in Warsaw's schools, Marya's father, a teacher, kept his laboratory equipment at home. Marya developed an early interest in science.

Marya Sklodovska, later married and known as Marie Curie, would become one of the world's most famous and important scientists. Her discoveries would have been outstanding at any time, but she made them at a time when women very rarely studied science to an advanced level or worked as scientists. She received many awards and honours which had never been given to a woman before. She overcame enormous difficulties to do the work that was most important to her. She could have made a great deal of money from the fruits of her work, but she made her discoveries freely available for the good of science. She discovered new materials that behaved in strange ways. By studying them, she opened up a completely new branch of science that led to nuclear power stations, radiation treatments for cancer and a huge advance in our understanding of atoms.

A Polish girl

Marya Sklodovska, the girl who would become Marie Curie, grew up with her father's laboratory equipment all around her at home. Perhaps it triggered her interest in science. She was a star pupil at school. When she left she wanted to study medicine at university, but it was not possible in Warsaw. She would have to leave home.

In 1891, she moved to Paris to study and called herself Marie. She had a lot of catching up to do to match the other students. She worked very hard and was awarded degrees in physics and maths. Then she met a scientist called Pierre Curie. Pierre and Marie were married within a year. The new Madame Curie decided to study for another degree, a doctorate in science. It was something that no woman in Europe had ever done before!

Atoms

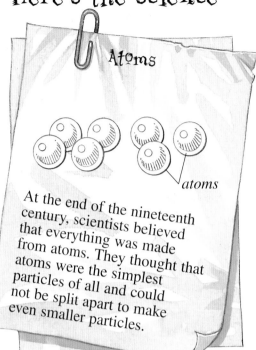

atoms

At the end of the nineteenth century, scientists believed that everything was made from atoms. They thought that atoms were the simplest particles of all and could not be split apart to make even smaller particles.

GOVERNESS. Before she could go to Paris to study, Marya earned money by teaching and working as a governess for wealthy families (above).

MARRIAGE. Marie and Pierre Curie were married in Paris on 26th July, 1895. They spent the rest of the summer touring the countryside on their bicycles.

I understand what's happening now, Dad.

Invisible rays

Marie had to decide what to study for her doctorate. Two recent discoveries interested her. Two scientists, Wilhelm Roentgen and Henri Becquerel, had discovered mysterious rays. Roentgen's rays were later called X-rays. They could pass through someone and make a shadow picture of their bones! Roentgen made an X-ray photograph of his wife's hand. Becquerel discovered that a material called uranium gave out rays that darkened photographic plates too. Most scientists were more interested in X-rays, but Marie decided to study uranium rays. Her decision would change the history of science.

Becquerel's uranium rays

BECQUEREL PLACED a piece of uranium on top of a photographic plate wrapped in paper to keep light out.

AFTER SOME TIME, he unwrapped the plate and, in darkness, processed it in a bath of chemicals.

WHEN HE HELD the plate up to the light, he could see a dark smudge in the middle where the uranium had been.

Look, darling, the magic of X-rays!

Rutherford's atom

Some scientists thought atoms might be dotted with negatively-charged particles called electrons.

Electrons

In 1907, experiments carried out by Ernest Rutherford showed that atoms might be made of a small, positively-charged nucleus in the middle, surrounded by negatively-charged electrons. The electrons flew around the nucleus.

Nucleus

LEAD UNDERWEAR. When people found out about X-rays, some of them were worried that an X-ray machine might be able to see through their clothes. A few actually wore lead underwear to block the rays!

Lead underwear

A mystery element

Marie Curie wondered if uranium was the only material that produced mysterious rays. To find out, she would have to test hundreds of different materials. Other scientists did this by checking whether the materials darkened photographic plates. Marie chose a different method that was faster and more accurate. She tested each material by placing it inside an instrument, called an electrometer, invented by her husband. Any rays it produced made it easier for electricity to flow through the instrument.

This one is very interesting, Marie!

The size of the electric current showed the strength of the rays. Most of the tests showed no activity, but materials containing an element called thorium produced rays just like uranium. Marie invented a new word to describe the ray-making behaviour of these materials – radioactivity.

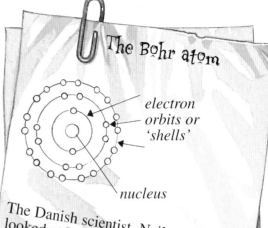

The Bohr atom

electron
orbits or
'shells'

nucleus

The Danish scientist, Neils Bohr, looked at Rutherford's idea of what an atom was like and improved it. He thought electrons might only be allowed at certain distances from the nucleus, like moons orbiting a planet, instead of swarming randomly around it.

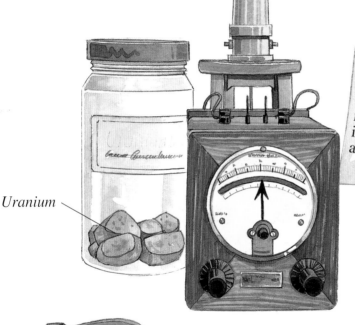

Uranium

PITCHBLENDE. One material tested by Marie Curie was pitchblende. It contains uranium, but it produced even stronger rays than uranium. There had to be something else in it making the rays. She found two new elements. She called one 'polonium', after her native Poland, and the other 'radium'.

Pitchblende

A witch's brew

Marie and Pierre needed a lot more radium, but pitchblende was too expensive for them to buy. Fortunately, the Austrian government, who had spare radioactive material, gave them a tonne of it and let them buy more cheaply. They worked in an old shed with a leaking roof – they had to be careful where they put equipment to avoid drips when it rained! They boiled the pitchblende with acids and other chemicals to separate its radioactive part from the rest. The shed quickly filled up with smoke and fumes, so they worked outside whenever possible. Their shelves were soon full of jars of liquids and solids produced by processing the pitchblende. They had to process about 8 tonnes of pitchblende to produce just 1 gram of radium!

Radioactive decay

Nucleus

When Marie Curie invented the word radioactivity to describe the strange ray-making behaviour of radium, no-one really knew what it was. One idea was that it might be particles or energy flying out of the nucleus in the middle of an atom.

ENDLESS STIRRING. Marie stirred her 'witch's brew' of smelly chemicals and pitchblende, while Pierre tested the different solids and liquids her work produced.

Getting to know radium

When Marie studied radium, she found that its radiation was two million times stronger than that of uranium. It emitted a radioactive gas, later called radon. It also gave off heat and glowed in the dark brightly enough to read by. It could make nearby materials glow too. Diamond glowed particularly well. It also darkened photographic plates, just like uranium. It changed the colour of the glass bottles it was put in, turning clear glass to violet. Radium also made nearby materials radioactive, including Marie Curie's own clothes!

— *Radium*

HOT STUFF. Radium gave off so much heat that if it was dropped into some cold water, it could make the water boil (left)!

KEEPING WARM. Marie's shed was often freezing cold. Any heat, even from a tiny bottle of radium, was very welcome indeed!

Brrrrr

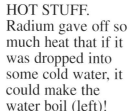

14

The radium craze

When news of radium started spreading, it fascinated everyone. Newspapers and magazines claimed that the glowing liquid could treat pain, cure all sorts of diseases, make amazing machines work or even destroy a whole city with its great power! Medicines containing radium were soon on sale to the public. It was several years before people found out how dangerous it was. Both Marie and Pierre had become ill during their work. They had lost weight and their fingers were sore from handling radium and other radioactive materials with their bare hands.

The Miracle of RADIUM

You look radiant this evening!

MIRACLE MEDICINE. People thought radium was a miracle material that could cure illnesses. They were soon buying radium medicines.

RADIUM PARTIES. At parties, girls sometimes painted radium on their nails to make them glow in the dark! Sometimes they even mixed radium with drinks to make them glow! They had no idea how dangerous the radiation from radium was and how it could harm them.

I've painted my toenails, too!

Isotopes

Electron
Proton

Scientists discovered that there are different forms of the same element, some heavier than others. These different forms are called isotopes. There are three isotopes of hydrogen – with one, two or three particles in its nucleus.

1 proton
1 neutron

1 proton
2 neutrons

DANGER! Girls who painted clock faces with radium often put their brush between their lips to form a point on it. When their teeth started falling out, doctors traced the problem to radium.

Blisters and burns

few scientists had noticed that radioactive materials could be harmful. They could cause burns. When Henri Becquerel carried some radium in his pocket, it burned his side. Marie Curie was also burned when carrying some radium, even though it was inside a metal box! Pierre studied radium's effect by carrying out a very dangerous experiment on himself! He put some radium on his arm and then watched what it did to his skin! He wondered if radium's ability to kill cells might be used to treat some illnesses. If it could kill living cells, then it could kill diseased cells. Perhaps radium could treat cancer, a condition caused by cells multiplying out of control. When doctors tried it, it worked. Radiotherapy, as it became known, is still used today to treat some types of cancer.

The things I do in the name of science!

SOON AFTER Pierre put some radium on his arm, the skin started turning red, like a burn, but it was not very painful.

THE REDNESS got worse over the next few days. By the twentieth day, scabs had formed over the bright red skin.

IT CONTINUED getting worse and changed into an open wound. It was so bad that it had to be dressed with bandages.

FINALLY, new skin started forming over the wound on day 42. Ten days later, it had healed, but it looked a strange grey colour.

DNA damage

The genetic code that controls all living cells is made from DNA. DNA is a long coiled-up string of particles. Radiation harms living cells, because it knocks particles out of the DNA. This may kill the cells or just change the way they work.

Radiation

DNA strand

TREATING CANCER. Tiny glass tubes full of radioactive radon gas collected from radium were used to treat patients suffering from cancer. The radiation killed the cancer cells.

19

Spreading the word

n 1903, Marie and Pierre Curie were invited to London to speak about their work to the Royal Institution, a very important organisation of the most famous British scientists. At that time, women were not allowed to speak at the Royal Institution. Pierre had to give the talk while Marie looked on. In fact, Marie was the first woman ever to be allowed into a meeting there at all! Pierre explained everything that they had found out about radium. He brought some radium with him and used it to show its strange effects. Reports of the talk made the Curies famous all over Britain.

At the end of 1903, Henri Becquerel and the Curies were awarded the Nobel Prize for physics, one of the world's most important science awards. Sadly, Marie was too ill to make the 48-hour journey to Stockholm to collect the award from the King of Sweden. Many more honours and awards followed.

PIERRE FALLS ILL. Before his talk at the Royal Institution, Pierre was so ill from radioactive poisoning that he was hardly able to dress himself. During the talk, his fingers were so sore that he spilled some of the precious radium in the hall.

DAVY MEDAL. The many awards given to the Curies for their work included the Royal Society's Davy Medal. It is only given for the most important discoveries in the world of chemistry.

The Davy Medal

Transmutation

Protactinium 234 $^{234}_{91}Pa$ *

Beta particle emitted

β

Uranium 234 $^{234}_{92}U$

a

Thorium 230 $^{230}_{90}Th$

a

Radium 226 $^{226}_{88}Ra$

a

Radon 222 $^{222}_{86}Rn$

Alpha particle emitted

When an atom decays, the numbers and types of particles in its nucleus change. The atom changes from one element to another, called transmutation. Radium is produced by the decay of other elements.

So much money just wasted!

* This way of writing an element identifies which isotope it is.

INVITATIONS. Marie and Pierre were invited to dine with important and wealthy people. They often wondered how much equipment they could have bought for their laboratory with all the fine jewellery the guests wore.

Tragedy

O n 19th April, 1906, tragedy struck. Pierre was run over by a horse-drawn wagon as he crossed the road. He was killed instantly. Marie was heart-broken. Pierre had been a professor at the Sorbonne, part of the University of Paris. The Sorbonne asked Marie if she would take his place. She accepted and so became the first woman ever to work as a professor at the Sorbonne. Then the University of Paris and the Pasteur Institute agreed to build a Radium Institute, with a radioactivity laboratory headed by Marie.

Marie and Pierre Curie had been awarded their first Noble Prize for their work on radioactivity. In 1911, Marie was awarded an amazing second Nobel Prize, this time for chemistry. It was given to her for her discovery of radium and polonium.

Whaaooooo, boys!

Here's the science

Measuring radiation

To measure things, there have to be units, such as metres and kilograms. New units were needed to measure radioactivity. Marie was given the honour of creating one of these new units. Scientists named it the 'curie' in her honour. One curie is the amount of a radioactive element in which there are 37 thousand million atomic disintegrations every second.

TEACHING. Marie and some of her friends taught classes for young children. Her daughter, Irene, and the other children were taught science by the world's leading expert on radioactivity!

The 'Little Curies'

The Radium Institute was completed in 1914 on the newly-named Rue Pierre-Curie, but Marie could not move in. World War I had begun and her staff had been called up for military service. Marie took all of France's radium out of Paris to keep it out of German hands. She took it to Bordeaux by train. Then she had vans fitted with X-ray equipment and set off for the battle-front with her daughter, Irene. French soldiers called the vans 'les petites Curies' (the little Curies). She took X-rays of wounded soldiers to help the doctors who were treating them. Soon after the war ended in 1918, she was finally able to move into the Radium Institute.

No, dear – it's not my lunchbox.

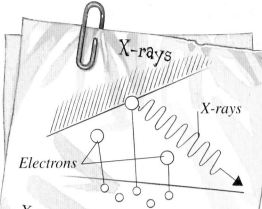

X-rays

X-rays

Electrons

X-rays are produced when very fast-moving electrons hit a hard material and stop suddenly. Their movement is instantly changed into energy waves, like radio waves but much shorter. The waves have so much energy that they can pass through some things, including people's bodies!

THE WAR EFFORT. The government asked people to give gold and silver for the war. Marie tried to donate her medals, but officials refused to take them.

Welcome to America

In May 1920, Marie gave an interview to an American magazine editor, Mrs William Brown Meloney. When Marie told her how badly she needed more radium, Mrs Meloney started the Marie Curie Radium Campaign to get it for her. France offered her the Legion of Honour, the country's most important award, but she refused to accept it. She wanted a better laboratory, not more awards. Although she hated publicity and crowds, she was persuaded to go on a tour of the USA in 1921. It was a great success. The US President, Warren Harding, met her and gave her more radium. Many other people offered help too. She returned to Paris with radium, equipment and money. She made a second tour of the USA in 1929 and met the new US President, Herbert Hoover. This tour raised enough to set up a second Radium Institute in Warsaw headed by her sister, Bronya.

Vive la France!

ACHES AND PAINS. Within a few days of arriving in the USA, Marie had to put her right arm in a sling, because her hand and arm were aching from shaking hands with so many people!

Here's the science

Half-life

1,620 years   1,620 years

Some elements decay faster than others. The speed is given by an element's half-life – the time for half of it to decay. A half-life can be less than a second or thousands of years. One of radium's isotopes has a half-life of 1,620 years.

Welcome to America!

DEGREES. Universities and colleges all over the USA gave Marie degrees to honour her work. When she was too ill to receive them in person, her daughters, Irene and Eve, accepted them for her.

The end of the story

Marie's health had been worsening for years. She had painful burns on her hands. She felt tired and often suffered from fevers and chills. Her sight was failing too. She wrote her notes in huge letters and her daughters had to guide her around. After an operation on her eyes, she was able to work again and even drive a car. Thirty-five years of handling radioactive materials and breathing in radioactive gases without any protection, as well as exposure to X-rays during the war, had taken its toll. On some days, she was too ill to work.

Doctors were unable to find out what was wrong with Marie. They thought her ill health might be caused by tuberculosis. Then blood tests showed she was suffering from a blood disorder, but they did not know what it was. It was probably leukaemia, a type of cancer that affects the blood, and it was probably caused by radiation.

You must rest more, Mother.

LEAD SCREENS. In 1925, the French Academy of Medicine advised everyone working with radium to have blood tests and use lead screens for safety. Marie insisted that her students and staff take all safety measures, but she did not use them herself.

Protective lead outfit for handling radioactive material

FINAL DAYS. In May 1934, Marie left the laboratories of the Radium Institute for the last time. Her condition gradually worsened. Doctors were unable to do anything more for her. She died on 4th July, 1934, with her daughter, Eve, by her bedside.

Here's the science

The effect on life

Different types of radiation have different effects on living things, including people. So, knowing how much radiation there is does not tell you how much, or how little, it will affect living things. Being able to measure the real effects of radiation is very important when it comes to protecting people from it. For this, a unit called the sievert was created.

REBURIAL. In 1995, Marie and Pierre Curie were re-buried in the Panthéon in Paris, the burial place of France's most famous people.

Glossary

Alpha particle A type of particle given out by some radioactive elements. It is made from four smaller particles – two protons and two neutrons.

Atom The smallest particle of an element that can take part in a chemical reaction.

Beta particle A type of particle given out by some radioactive elements. A beta particle is an electron produced when a neutron decays, leaving a proton behind.

Cancer An illness caused by cells multiplying out of control. Cancer can be caused by the damaging effects of radiation on living cells.

Decay The change of a radioactive nucleus into a different nucleus by giving out particles or energy waves, resulting in a new isotope.

Electron One of the three particles that atoms are made from. An electron has a negative electric charge.

Element The simplest form of a substance that can take part in chemical reactions.

Gamma ray One type of radiation given out by a radioactive nucleus in the form of a wave, like radio or light, but with much shorter waves.

Half-life The time for half of the atoms of a radioactive element to decay once.

Isotopes Different forms of the same element made from atoms with different numbers of neutrons in their nucleus. Some isotopes are radioactive.

Laboratory A place where scientists work and carry out experiments.

Leukaemia A type of cancer that affects the blood. More and more white blood cells are produced while the number of red blood cells falls.

Atomic mass The total number of protons and neutrons in the nucleus.

Neutron One of the three particles that atoms are made from. Neutrons are found inside an atom's nucleus. Not all atoms have neutrons. A neutron has no electric charge. A neutron can change into a proton by giving out a beta particle.

Nucleus The particle, or particles, at the centre of an atom.

Pitchblende A type of rock that contains uranium. Marie Curie discovered radium and polonium in this material.

Polonium One of the two new elements discovered by Marie Curie in pitchblende.

Proton One of the three particles that atoms are made from. Protons are found inside an atom's nucleus. A proton has a positive electric charge.

Radiation The particles and wave energy given out by a radioactive substance. Other waves, including radio, light and X-rays, are also called radiation.

Radioactivity The breakdown of a radioactive element by giving out alpha or beta particles or gamma rays.

Radium One of the two new elements discovered by Marie Curie in pitchblende.

Transmutation The change of one type of atom to another by radioactive decay.

Tumour A growth caused by cells dividing and multiplying out of control.

X-rays Energy waves similar to radio waves and light waves but much shorter, produced when fast-moving electrons hit a hard material.

Index

A
alpha particles 15, 21, 30
atoms 7, 9, 11, 13, 21, 30

B
Becquerel, Henri 8, 18, 20
beta particles 15, 21, 30
Bohr, Niels 11

C
cancer 18, 19, 30
curie (unit of measurement) 23

D
Davy Medal 21
DNA 19

E
electrons 9, 11, 17, 25, 30
element 17, 21, 23, 27, 30

G
gamma rays 15, 30

H
half-life 27, 30
Harding, President Warren 26
Hoover, President Herbert 26
hydrogen 17

I
isotopes 17, 30

L
lead underwear 9
Legion of Honour 26
leukaemia 28, 31
Little Curies, The 24

M
Marie Curie Radium Campaign 26
medicine 16
Meloney, Mrs William Brown 26

N
neutrons 17
Nobel Prize 20, 23
nucleus 9, 11, 13, 15

P
Panthéon, The 29
Pasteur Institute 22
pitchblende 11, 12, 13
polonium 11, 23
protactinium 21
protons 17

R
radiation 14, 15, 19, 28
radioactive decay 13
radioactivity 11, 13, 22, 23
radiotherapy 18
radium 11-14, 16-21, 23, 24, 26, 27, 29

Radium Institute 22, 24, 26, 29
radon 21
Roentgen, Wilhelm 8
Royal Institution 20
Royal Society 21
Rutherford, Ernest 9

S
sievert (unit of measurement) 29
Sorbonne, The 22

T
thorium 11, 21
transmutation 21
tuberculosis 28

U
University of Paris 22
uranium 8, 10, 11, 14, 21

X
X-rays 8, 9, 24, 25, 28

To read more about the fascinating life of Marie Curie and the legacy of her research, try these internet links:
www.aip.org/history/curie
www.mariecurie.org.uk
DON'T FORGET TO ASK PERMISSION AT HOME OR IN SCHOOL BEFORE USING THE INTERNET.